A MINCED UP!

THE ULTIMATE IN FAST & FRUGAL FEASTS!

LOVE FOOD™

This edition published by Parragon Books Ltd in 2014
LOVE FOOD is an imprint of Parragon Books Ltd

Parragon Books Ltd
Chartist House
15–17 Trim Street
Bath BA1 1HA, UK
www.parragon.com/lovefood

ISBN: 978-1-4723-2982-0

Printed in China

New recipes written by Beverly Le Blanc
Introduction and incidental text by Anne Sheasby
New internal photography by Clive Streeter
New internal home economy by Theresa Goldfinch
New cover photography by Mike Cooper
Additional design work by Geoff Borin and Siân Williams
Internal illustrations by Nicola O'Byrne and Julie Ingham

Notes for the Reader
This book uses both metric and imperial measurements. Follow the same units of measurement throughout; do not mix metric and imperial. All spoon measurements are level: teaspoons are assumed to be 5 ml, and tablespoons are assumed to be 15 ml. Unless otherwise stated, milk is assumed to be full fat, eggs and individual vegetables are medium, and pepper is freshly ground black pepper. Unless otherwise stated, all root vegetables should be peeled prior to using.

Garnishes, decorations and serving suggestions are all optional and not necessarily included in the recipe ingredients or method. The times given are an approximate guide only. Preparation times differ according to the techniques used by different people and the cooking times may also vary from those given. Optional ingredients, variations or serving suggestions have not been included in the time calculations.

Picture acknowledgements
Cover illustrations courtesy of iStock

ALL
MINCED
UP!

CONTENTS

BREAKING GROUND

Minced meat is suitable for making a wide range of delicious recipes from all over the world, many of which are hearty and homely, some of which are thrifty or frugal, but all of which are full of flavour.

Minced meat is available in several types and is ideal for creating tasty dishes that are economical too. Varieties of mince include beef, pork, lamb, turkey, chicken, venison and veal.

Mince is made from various parts of the animal, usually the cheaper cuts, and it is generally inexpensive, but it can vary enormously in quality and fat content and this will be partly reflected in the price. Butcher's minced beef, for example, may also contain trimmings from more expensive cuts of beef. Fresh minced

meat is widely available from outlets such as supermarkets, butchers and farm shops, and many butchers will mince meat fresh for you to order, if required. Some types of minced meat can also be bought ready-frozen.

Minced pork and lamb are also readily available and can be used in a wide variety of recipes. Minced chicken is obtainable but is not so easy to find, whereas minced turkey is readily available as turkey mince or lean turkey breast mince. Other minced meats such as venison and veal may not be so widely obtainable, but some supermarkets and other outlets, including butchers and online suppliers, stock these more readily now too.

Minced red meat is a good source of protein, and depending on the quality of mince you buy, the fat and saturated fat contents vary. Minced turkey and chicken are low in fat and are a good source of protein

and can provide a lighter, healthier alternative to minced beef when made into dishes such as burgers and meatballs.

Mycoprotein mince is also available to buy as fresh or frozen mince. Mycoprotein is a meat-free form of high quality protein, suitable for vegetarians (however, it is not suitable for vegans as it contains a little egg to help with binding). It is low in fat and saturated fats, low in sodium and it contains no cholesterol. It is also a good source of dietary fibre. This vegetarian alternative to mince can be used to create many flavourful family recipes, including chilli, burgers, lasagne and spaghetti bolognese, as well as many other mince favourites.

COMFORTING EATS

CREAMY CHICKEN HASH

SERVES: 4–6 **PREP TIME: 10 MINS** **COOK TIME: 15–20 MINS**

INGREDIENTS

3 tbsp sunflower oil

450 g/1 lb fresh chicken mince

1 tsp dried thyme or dried dill

pinch of cayenne pepper

1 onion, finely chopped

1 large red pepper, deseeded and finely chopped

2 large garlic cloves, finely chopped

2 tbsp plain flour

300 ml/10 fl oz milk

100 g/3½ oz frozen peas

200 g/7 oz canned sweetcorn kernels, drained and rinsed

salt and pepper

1. Heat 2 tablespoons of the oil in a large frying pan over a medium-high heat. Add the chicken, thyme, cayenne pepper, and salt and pepper to taste and fry, stirring with a wooden spoon to break up the chicken into large clumps, for 4–6 minutes until just starting to brown. Transfer to a bowl using a slotted spoon and set aside.

2. Add the remaining oil to the pan, then add the onion and red pepper and fry, stirring, for 3–5 minutes until the onion is soft. Add the garlic and stir for a further 30 seconds.

3. Sprinkle over the flour and stir for about 1 minute. Slowly stir in the milk and continue stirring until a smooth, creamy sauce forms.

4. Return the chicken to the pan and add the peas and sweetcorn. Bring to the boil, stirring, then reduce the heat and simmer, uncovered, for 5 minutes, or until the peas are tender. Adjust the salt and pepper, if necessary. Serve immediately.

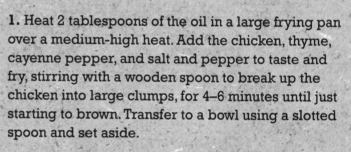

CHICKEN-STUFFED SQUASH

SERVES: 4　　　**PREP TIME: 20 MINS**　　　**COOK TIME: 1 HR**

INGREDIENTS

2 butternut squash, about
500 g/1 lb 2 oz each, halved
lengthways, deseeded, all the
fibres removed and the flesh
slashed in a criss-cross pattern

3 tbsp garlic-flavoured olive oil
or plain olive oil

450 g/1 lb fresh chicken mince

1 red onion, finely chopped

½ tsp dried red chilli flakes,
or to taste

100 g/3½ oz baby spinach
leaves

freshly grated nutmeg, to taste

4 tbsp toasted pine nuts

100 g/3½ oz feta cheese,
drained and crumbled

2 tbsp chopped fresh parsley

salt and pepper

salad leaves, to serve

1. Preheat the oven to 200°C/400°F/Gas Mark 6. Rub 1 tablespoon of the oil over the squash halves, place them on a baking sheet, cut side up, and roast in the preheated oven for 45 minutes, or until tender.

2. Meanwhile, heat the remaining oil in a saucepan over a medium–high heat. Add the chicken, onion, chilli flakes, and salt and pepper to taste and fry, stirring with a wooden spoon to break up the chicken into large clumps, for 4–6 minutes until cooked through.

3. Add the spinach and nutmeg, increase the heat and stir until the liquid from the spinach evaporates. Transfer to a bowl and set aside.

4. Remove the squash from the oven (do not switch off the oven) and leave until cool enough to handle.

5. Scoop out the squash flesh, retaining a thin shell. Finely chop the flesh and add to the bowl with the remaining ingredients. Toss together and adjust the seasoning, if necessary.

6. Divide the stuffing between the hollowed-out squash halves. Return to the oven for 10 minutes, or until the cheese is melted. Serve with salad leaves.

BACON-WRAPPED CHICKEN BURGERS

MAKES: 4

PREP TIME: 10 MINS PLUS CHILLING

COOK TIME: 10–15 MINS

INGREDIENTS

450 g/1 lb fresh chicken mince
1 onion, grated
2 garlic cloves, crushed
55 g/2 oz pine nuts, toasted
55 g/2 oz Gruyère cheese, grated
2 tbsp snipped fresh chives
2 tbsp wholemeal flour
8 slices lean back bacon
1–2 tbsp sunflower oil
salt and pepper

TO SERVE

4 crusty rolls, split
red onion slices
lettuce leaves
4 tbsp mayonnaise
spring onions, chopped

1. Place the chicken mince, onion, garlic, pine nuts, Gruyère cheese, chives and salt and pepper to taste in a food processor or blender. Using the pulse button, blend the mixture together using short sharp bursts. Scrape out onto a board and shape into four even-sized burgers. Coat in the flour, then cover and chill in the refrigerator for 1 hour.

2. Wrap each burger with two bacon slices, securing in place with a wooden cocktail stick.

3. Heat a heavy-based frying pan over a medium heat and add the oil. When hot, add the burgers and cook over a medium heat for 5–6 minutes on each side, or until cooked through and the juices run clear.

4. Serve the burgers in the crusty rolls with the red onion, lettuce, a spoonful of mayonnaise and spring onions. Serve immediately.

HERO TIPS

You can alter the flavour and texture of these luscious burgers by replacing the pine nuts with flaked almonds or unsalted cashews. If using whole nuts, chop them first and, if liked, toast lightly.

TURKEY POT PIE

SERVES: 4   **PREP TIME: 20 MINS**   **COOK TIME: APPROX. 1 HR**

INGREDIENTS

125 g/4½ oz French beans, topped, tailed and roughly chopped

1 large carrot, diced

2 bay leaves

2 tbsp sunflower oil

400 g/14 oz fresh turkey mince

1 leek, thinly sliced

125 g/4½ oz chestnut mushrooms, trimmed and sliced

4 spring onions, finely chopped

1 tsp dried tarragon

3 tbsp plain flour

5 tbsp milk

1 small egg, beaten

225 g/8 oz ready-rolled shortcrust pastry, thawed if frozen

sesame seeds, for sprinkling

salt and pepper

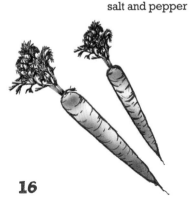

1. Preheat the oven to 190°C/375°F/Gas Mark 5. Bring a large saucepan of lightly salted water to the boil, add the beans, carrot and bay leaves and blanch for 3 minutes, or until tender-crisp. Strain, reserving 5 tablespoons of the cooking liquid and discarding the bay leaves.

2. Meanwhile, heat the oil in a frying pan over a medium-high heat. Add the turkey and leek and fry, stirring with a wooden spoon to break up the meat into large clumps, for 3 minutes, or until it loses its raw appearance. Add the mushrooms, and salt and pepper to taste and stir until the mushrooms absorb the liquid they give off. Stir in the spring onions, tarragon, carrots and beans.

3. Sprinkle over the flour and stir for 1 minute. Stir in the milk and reserved cooking liquid and bring to the boil. Reduce the heat and simmer for 2 minutes. Adjust the seasoning.

4. Spoon the mixture into a 1.2-litre/2-pint pie dish and brush the rim with egg. Add the pastry, press around the edges to seal, then trim. Brush the top with beaten egg, sprinkle with sesame seeds and cut a hole in the centre. Place on a baking sheet and bake in the preheated oven for 40 minutes, or until golden brown. Serve immediately.

DAILY GRIND!

Minced meat or mince (also called ground meat) is simply meat that has been finely chopped or broken down into smaller pieces by passing it through a mincing machine or meat grinder. The term also occasionally refers to meat (such as steak) that has been finely chopped using a sharp knife.

You can buy different types of minced meat, but you can also mince or grind your own meat at home, if you have some basic equipment. Mincing your own meat allows you to know the provenance of your mince and to control the quality, freshness, choice and type of cuts going into your mince.

If you plan to mince your own meat on a regular basis, then it's worth investing in a decent meat grinder. A meat grinder or meat mincer is a kitchen appliance that finely chops raw meat or poultry. Meat grinders vary, but the basic principle and mechanism used to grind the meat is similar. There are several types of meat grinder available from the classic, cast-iron, manual/hand-cranked grinder, to the more sophisticated stand-alone electric

meat mincers or grinders, and prices vary quite a bit. You can also buy meat grinder attachments for some electric stand mixers. Always follow the manufacturer's guidelines on assembling and operating the meat grinder, as well as the safety and cleaning tips given. Read through the instructions before use.

You can also 'mince' or finely chop meat using a food processor fitted with the metal blade, but you need to be careful not to over-process the meat into mush (using the pulse button in short bursts is the best way to do this), and be sure to process the diced meat in small batches.

If you are mincing meat at home, you can choose any boneless cut of meat, depending on the recipe you are preparing it for. Try experimenting with different cuts of meat. It's good to use cuts that have some visible fat, otherwise if you use meat that is very lean it is likely to dry out and not be as flavourful, but be sure to trim off any tough connective tissue or sinew (and remove most of the fat) before grinding. It's also best to use well-chilled meat for grinding as it is firmer and will be easier to grind. Some manufacturers also recommend chilling the meat in the freezer for a short time (30 minutes or so) before grinding.

As a general guide, for minced beef, suitable cuts include neck, skirt, flank, shin and chuck, blade or braising steak. For minced lamb, suitable cuts include scrag end, neck fillet, shoulder and breast. For minced pork, suitable cuts include leg and lean belly, and for minced venison, suitable cuts include flank and neck.

If you use leaner cuts of meat, you may need to add some meat fat or a percentage of fattier meat so that the minced meat doesn't dry out too much during cooking. A little fat also adds flavour as well as juiciness to the cooked meat, especially when making recipes such as burgers.

Before you begin, cut the meat into small chunks or cubes (about 2.5 cm/1 inch) to make it easier to grind more quickly, easily and uniformly.

Grind the meat in batches as directed in the manufacturers guidelines. Once ground, either use the mince immediately or store it in a covered or airtight container in the refrigerator and use within 1–2 days.

To prepare your own minced chicken or turkey, use skinless boneless chicken breasts or turkey breast fillets or boneless thigh meat. Remove any tendons or pieces of fat, then cut the meat into 2.5-cm/1-inch cubes. Either use a meat grinder to grind the chicken or turkey, or place it in a food processor and pulse in short bursts until the meat is finely or coarsely chopped, depending on your requirements, but do not over-process the meat. Once ground, use immediately or store as above.

Always wash your hands thoroughly before and after handling raw (or cooked) meat or poultry. Once you have finished grinding your meat, take the grinder apart and wash it thoroughly in hot soapy water, then carefully dry it as best you can, before allowing the parts to air dry completely before storing. Make sure work surfaces and all other utensils used are also cleaned with hot soapy water, and disinfect worktops after use, preferably with a mild detergent or an antibacterial cleaner.

BEEF & BEAN SOUP

SERVES: 6   **PREP TIME: 20 MINS**   **COOK TIME: 40 MINS**

INGREDIENTS

2 tbsp vegetable oil
1 large onion, finely chopped
2 garlic cloves, finely chopped
1 green pepper,
deseeded and sliced
2 carrots, sliced
400 g/14 oz canned
black eyed beans
225 g/8 oz fresh beef mince
1 tsp each ground cumin, chilli
powder and paprika
¼ cabbage, sliced
225 g/8 oz tomatoes, peeled
and chopped
600 ml/1 pint beef stock
salt and pepper

1. Heat the oil in a large saucepan over a medium heat. Add the onion and garlic and cook, stirring frequently, for 5 minutes, or until softened. Add the pepper and carrots and cook for a further 5 minutes.

2. Meanwhile, drain the beans, reserving the liquid from the can. Place two thirds of the beans, reserving the remainder, in a food processor or blender with the bean liquid and process until smooth.

3. Add the beef to the saucepan and cook, stirring constantly, to break up any lumps, until well browned. Add the spices and cook, stirring, for 2 minutes. Add the cabbage, tomatoes, stock and puréed beans and season to taste with salt and pepper. Bring to the boil, then reduce the heat, cover and simmer for 15 minutes, or until the vegetables are tender.

4. Stir in the reserved beans, cover and simmer for a further 5 minutes. Ladle the soup into warmed bowls and serve immediately.

MEAL-IN-A-BOWL BEEF & HERB SOUP

SERVES: 6 **PREP TIME: 10 MINS** **COOK TIME: APPROX. 1 HR**

INGREDIENTS

- 2 onions
- 2 tbsp sunflower oil
- 1 tbsp ground turmeric
- 1 tsp ground cumin
- 100 g/3½ oz green or yellow split peas
- 1.2 litres/2 pints beef stock
- 225 g/8 oz fresh beef mince
- 200 g/7 oz long-grain rice
- 1 tbsp chopped fresh coriander, plus extra to garnish
- 1 tbsp snipped fresh chives
- 55 g/2 oz baby spinach, finely chopped
- 25 g/1 oz butter
- 2 garlic cloves, finely chopped
- 3 tbsp chopped fresh mint
- salt and pepper
- Greek-style yogurt, to serve

1. Grate one of the onions into a bowl and finely chop the other. Heat the oil in a large saucepan. Add the chopped onion and cook over a low–medium heat, stirring occasionally, for 8–10 minutes, until golden. Stir in the turmeric and cumin, add the split peas and pour in the stock. Bring to the boil, then reduce the heat, cover and simmer for 15 minutes.

2. Meanwhile, add the beef to the grated onion, season to taste with salt and pepper and mix well. Shape the mixture into small balls.

3. Add the meatballs to the soup, re-cover the pan and simmer for a further 10 minutes. Add the rice and stir in the coriander, chives and spinach. Simmer, stirring frequently, for 25–30 minutes, until the rice is tender.

4. Melt the butter in a frying pan. Add the garlic and cook over a low heat, stirring frequently, for 2–3 minutes. Stir in the mint and cook for a further minute.

5. Transfer the soup to warmed bowls and sprinkle over the garlic mixture. Serve immediately with Greek-style yogurt and garnished with coriander.

MEATLOAF

There are many versions of this well-loved American staple. This one uses a glaze that is not only delicious but also helps keep the meat wonderfully moist.

SERVES: 6–8

PREP TIME: 20 MINS PLUS RESTING

COOK TIME: APPROX. 1½ HRS

INGREDIENTS

25 g/1 oz butter

1 tbsp olive oil, plus extra for brushing

3 garlic cloves, chopped

100 g/3½ oz carrots, very finely diced

55 g/2 oz celery, very finely diced

1 onion, very finely diced

1 red pepper, deseeded and very finely diced

4 large white mushrooms, very finely diced

1 tsp dried thyme

2 tsp finely chopped rosemary

1 tsp Worcestershire sauce

6 tbsp tomato ketchup

½ tsp cayenne pepper

1.1 kg/2 lb 8 oz fresh beef mince, chilled

2 eggs, beaten

55 g/2 oz fresh breadcrumbs

2 tbsp brown sugar

1 tbsp Dijon mustard

salt and pepper

1. Melt the butter with the oil and garlic in a large frying pan. Add the vegetables and cook over a medium heat, stirring frequently, for 10 minutes until most of the moisture has evaporated.

2. Remove from the heat and stir in the herbs, Worcestershire sauce, 4 tablespoons of tomato ketchup and cayenne pepper. Leave to cool.

3. Preheat the oven to 160°C/325°F/Gas Mark 3. Brush a loaf tin with oil.

4. Put the beef into a large bowl and gently break it up with your fingertips. Add the vegetable mixture, eggs and salt and pepper to taste and mix gently with your fingers. Add the breadcrumbs and mix.

5. Transfer the meatloaf mixture to the loaf tin. Smooth the surface and bake in the preheated oven for 30 minutes.

6. Meanwhile, make a glaze by whisking together the sugar, the remaining 2 tablespoons of tomato ketchup, mustard and a pinch of salt.

7. Remove the meatloaf from the oven (do not switch off) and spread the glaze evenly over the top. Return to the oven and bake for a further 35–45 minutes. To check the meatloaf is cooked through, cut into the middle to check that the meat is no longer pink. Any juices that run out should be clear and piping hot with visible steam rising.

8. Remove from the oven and leave to rest for at least 15 minutes. Slice thickly to serve.

BEEF BURGERS

Burgers now come in many different flavours, shapes and sizes with something to suit all palates. This classic recipe uses just a small amount of chilli and a sprig of fresh basil to add an extra taste sensation.

MAKES: 4   **PREP TIME: 20 MINS**   **COOK TIME: 10–20 MINS**

INGREDIENTS

650 g/1 lb 7 oz fresh beef mince
1 red pepper, deseeded and finely chopped
1 garlic clove, finely chopped
2 small red chillies, deseeded and finely chopped
1 tbsp chopped fresh basil
½ tsp ground cumin
salt and pepper
fresh basil sprigs, to garnish
burger buns, to serve

1. Preheat the grill to medium–high. Put the beef, red pepper, garlic, chillies, chopped basil and cumin into a bowl.

2. Mix until well combined and season to taste with salt and pepper.

3. Using your hands, form the mixture into four burger shapes. Place the burgers under the preheated grill and cook for 5–8 minutes.

4. Using a spatula or fish slice, turn the burgers and cook on the other side for 5–8 minutes. To check the burgers are cooked through, cut into the middle to check that the meat is no longer pink. Any juices that run out should be clear and piping hot with visible steam rising.

5. Garnish with basil sprigs and serve immediately in burger buns.

HERO TIPS

Always handle the minced beef gently when shaping your burger patties. Over-working the meat will result in a tougher – and much less enjoyable – burger!

MINCED BEEF PIZZA

SERVES: 2   **PREP TIME: 20 MINS**   **COOK TIME: APPROX. 30 MINS**

INGREDIENTS

olive oil, for brushing and drizzling

175 g/6 oz fresh beef mince

1 small onion, finely chopped

1 garlic clove, finely chopped

1 tsp ground cumin

55 g/2 oz chargrilled red pepper in oil, drained and finely chopped

1 tbsp chopped fresh coriander

4 tbsp tomato purée

115 g/4 oz mozzarella cheese, sliced

salt and pepper

PIZZA DOUGH

175 g/6 oz self-raising flour, plus extra for dusting

pinch of salt

25 g/1 oz butter, cut into small pieces

100–125 ml/3½–4 fl oz milk

1. Preheat the oven to 200°C/400°F/Gas Mark 6. Brush a baking sheet with oil. To make the pizza dough, sift the flour and salt into a bowl. Add the butter and rub it in with your fingertips until the mixture resembles breadcrumbs. Pour in 100 ml/3½ fl oz of the milk and mix with a round-bladed knife to a soft dough, adding the remaining milk if necessary.

2. Turn out the dough onto a lightly floured surface and knead gently. Roll out to a 25-cm/10-inch round and transfer to the prepared baking sheet. Push up the edge slightly all around to make a rim.

3. Put the beef, onion, garlic and cumin in a non-stick frying pan and cook over a medium heat, stirring frequently and breaking up the meat with a wooden spoon, for 5–8 minutes, until evenly browned. Stir in the red pepper and coriander and season to taste with salt and pepper.

4. Spread the tomato purée over the pizza base. Cover with the beef mixture, top with the mozzarella and drizzle with oil. Bake in the preheated oven for 15–20 minutes, until the crust is crisp. Serve immediately.

BEEF FRIED RICE

SERVES: 6　　　　　**PREP TIME: 5 MINS**　　　　　**COOK TIME: 25–30 MINS**

INGREDIENTS

500 g/1 lb 2 oz long-grain rice
2 tbsp groundnut oil
4 large eggs, lightly beaten
650 g/1 lb 7 oz fresh beef mince
1 large onion, finely chopped
2 garlic cloves, finely chopped
140 g/5 oz frozen peas
3 tbsp light soy sauce
1 tsp sugar
salt
prawn crackers, to serve

1. Cook the rice in a large saucepan of salted boiling water for 15 minutes, until tender. Drain the rice, rinse with boiling water and set aside.

2. Heat a wok over a medium heat, then add the groundnut oil, swirl it around the wok and heat. Add the eggs and cook, stirring constantly, for 50–60 seconds, until set. Transfer to a dish and set aside.

3. Add the beef to the wok and stir-fry, breaking it up with a wooden spoon, for 4–5 minutes, until evenly browned. Stir in the onion, garlic and peas and stir-fry for a further 3–4 minutes.

4. Add the rice, soy sauce, sugar and eggs and cook, stirring constantly, for a further 1–2 minutes, until heated through. Serve immediately with prawn crackers.

HERO TIPS

This dish is perfect for using up left-over rice. You can also use any meat and any vegetables to hand, making it the ideal store-cupboard supper.

2

3

4

PORK & ROSEMARY BURGERS

A quick and easy alternative to the classic beef burger, this tasty pork version is beautifully flavoured with garlic and rosemary and makes for a fantastic treat any day of the week.

MAKES: 4

PREP TIME: 10 MINS

COOK TIME: APPROX. 10 MINS

INGREDIENTS

500 g/1 lb 2 oz fresh pork mince

1 small onion, finely chopped

1 garlic clove, crushed

1 tbsp finely chopped fresh rosemary

oil, for brushing

1 small French baguette, split and cut into four

2 tomatoes, sliced

4 gherkins, sliced

4 tbsp Greek-style yogurt

2 tbsp chopped fresh mint

salt and pepper

1. Use your hands to mix together the pork, onion, garlic and rosemary with salt and pepper to taste.

2. Divide the mixture into four and shape into flat burger shapes.

3. Brush a ridged griddle pan or frying pan with oil and cook the burgers for 6–8 minutes, turning once, until golden and cooked through.

4. Place a burger on the bottom half of each piece of baguette and top with the tomatoes and gherkins. Mix together the yogurt and mint.

5. Spoon the minty yogurt over the burgers and replace the baguette tops to serve.

1

2

4

33

PORK-STUFFED FLATBREADS

Ground allspice, cumin and coriander capture the warming flavours of the Middle East with these simple flatbreads. This recipe uses the classic thin, round flatbreads, but it works equally well with warmed pitta breads.

MAKES: 8

PREP TIME: 10 MINS PLUS STANDING

COOK TIME: 20 MINS

INGREDIENTS

1 red onion, halved and thinly sliced
2 tbsp olive oil
450 g/1 lb fresh pork mince
1 yellow onion, finely chopped
2 garlic cloves, finely chopped
1 tbsp tomato purée
1 tsp ground allspice
1 tsp ground coriander
1 tsp ground cumin
¼ tsp dried chilli flakes, or to taste
150 g/5½ oz feta cheese, drained and crumbled
2 tbsp chopped fresh coriander
salt and pepper

TO SERVE

8 flatbreads
sliced pickled chillies
Greek-style yogurt (optional)

1. Put the red onion into a non-metallic bowl, sprinkle with salt and set aside for 20 minutes to soften. Rinse well, then squeeze dry and set aside.

2. Heat the oil in a frying pan over a medium heat. Add the pork and yellow onion and fry, stirring to break up the meat, for 5 minutes, or until the pork is brown. Spoon off any excess fat.

3. Add the garlic, tomato purée, spices, chilli flakes, and salt and pepper to taste and stir for 1–3 minutes until the pork is cooked through. Stir in the cheese and chopped coriander.

4. Place the flatbreads, one at a time, in a large frying pan over a medium–high heat and heat until warmed through. Place one eighth of the filling along the centre and top with the red onions, pickled chillies, and a dollop of yogurt, if using.

5. Fold the flatbreads over to encase the filling and serve immediately, while still warm.

MEATBALL RISOTTO

SERVES: 4

PREP TIME: 20 MINS PLUS SOAKING

COOK TIME: 1 HR 15 MINS

INGREDIENTS

1 thick slice white bread, crusts removed

water or milk, for soaking

450 g/1 lb fresh pork mince

2 garlic cloves, very finely chopped

1 tbsp finely chopped onion

1 tsp black peppercorns, lightly crushed

pinch of salt

1 egg, lightly beaten

corn oil, for shallow-frying

400 g/14 oz canned chopped tomatoes

1 tbsp tomato purée

1 tsp dried oregano

1 tsp fennel seeds

pinch of sugar

1 litre/1¾ pints beef stock

1 tbsp olive oil

40 g/1½ oz butter

1 small onion, finely chopped

280 g/10 oz risotto rice

150 ml/5 fl oz red wine

salt and pepper

fresh basil leaves, to garnish

1. Place the bread into a bowl, add the water and leave to soak for 5 minutes. Squeeze out the water and place into a dry bowl together with the minced pork, garlic, onion, crushed peppercorns and salt. Add the egg and mix thoroughly. Shape the mixture into 16 equal-sized balls.

2. Heat the corn oil in a frying pan over a medium heat. Add the meatballs and cook for 5 minutes, or until cooked though. Remove and drain.

3. Combine the tomatoes, tomato purée, herbs and sugar in a heavy-based saucepan. Add the meatballs and bring to the boil. Reduce the heat and simmer for 30 minutes.

4. Bring the stock to a boil in a saucepan, then reduce the heat and keep simmering gently over a low heat while you are cooking the risotto.

5. Meanwhile, heat the olive oil with 25 g/1 oz of the butter in a deep saucepan until the butter has melted. Stir in the onion and cook for 5 minutes, until golden.

6. Reduce the heat, add the rice and mix to coat in oil and butter. Cook, stirring constantly, for 2–3 minutes, or until the grains are translucent. Add the wine and cook, stirring constantly until reduced.

7. Gradually add the simmering stock. Stir constantly and add more liquid as the rice absorbs each addition. Increase the heat so that the liquid bubbles. Cook for 20 minutes. Season to taste.

8. Lift out the cooked meatballs and add to the risotto. Remove the risotto from the heat and add the remaining butter. Mix well. Arrange the risotto and a few meatballs among 4 plates. Drizzle with the tomato sauce, garnish with the basil and serve.

SHEPHERD'S PIE

SERVES: 6   **PREP TIME: 10 MINS**   **COOK TIME: 1½ HRS**

INGREDIENTS
FILLING

1 tbsp olive oil

2 onions, finely chopped

2 garlic cloves, finely chopped

675 g/1 lb 8 oz fresh lamb mince

2 carrots, finely chopped

1 tbsp plain flour

225 ml/8 fl oz beef or chicken stock

125 ml/4 fl oz red wine

Worcestershire sauce (optional)

salt and pepper

MASHED POTATO TOPPING

675 g/1 lb 8 oz floury potatoes, such as King Edward, Maris Piper or Desirée, peeled and cut into chunks

55 g/2 oz butter

2 tbsp cream or milk

1. Preheat the oven to 180°C/350°F/Gas Mark 4. Heat the oil in a large flameproof casserole dish and fry the onions until softened, then add the garlic and stir well. Increase the heat and add the meat. Cook quickly to brown the meat all over, stirring continuously. Add the carrots and season well. Stir in the flour and add the stock and wine. Stir well and heat until simmering and thickened.

2. Cover the casserole dish and bake in the preheated oven for 1 hour. Check the consistency from time to time and add a little more stock or wine if required. The meat mixture should be quite thick but not dry. Season to taste and add a little Worcestershire sauce, if using.

3. Meanwhile, make the mashed potato topping. Bring a large saucepan of lightly salted water to the boil, add the potatoes and cook for 15–20 minutes. Drain well and mash with a potato masher until smooth. Season to taste and add the butter and cream, stirring until smooth.

4. Remove the casserole from the oven and increase the temperature to 200°C/400°F/Gas Mark 7. Spread or pipe the mashed potato on top of the mixture, return to the top of the oven and bake for a further 15-20 minutes, until golden brown. Serve immediately.

SPICE IT UP

WHITE CHILLI

White Chilli uses chicken mince instead of beef and cannellini beans rather than red kidney beans. To keep the chicken tender, avoid breaking it up into small pieces in step 1. It doesn't need to be completely cooked at this stage, as it continues to cook later in the recipe.

SERVES: 4   **PREP TIME: 10 MINS**   **COOK TIME: 25 MINS**

INGREDIENTS

2 tbsp sunflower oil

450 g/1 lb fresh chicken mince

1 large onion, chopped

2 large garlic cloves, finely chopped

2 tsp dried oregano

1 tsp dried thyme

1 tsp ground coriander

1 tsp ground cumin

½ tsp cayenne pepper, or to taste

400 g/14 oz canned cannellini beans, drained and rinsed

400 g/14 oz canned chopped tomatoes

125 ml/4 fl oz passata

½ tsp palm sugar or soft light brown sugar

salt and pepper

finely chopped fresh flat-leaf parsley, to garnish

cooked long-grain rice and soured cream (optional), to serve

1. Heat the oil in a saucepan over a medium–high heat. Add the chicken and onion and fry, stirring with a wooden spoon to break up the meat into large clumps, for 3–5 minutes until the onion is soft.

2. Add the garlic, oregano, thyme, coriander, cumin and cayenne pepper and fry for a further minute.

3. Add the beans, tomatoes, passata and sugar and season to taste with salt and pepper. Bring to the boil, stirring. Reduce the heat to low, cover and simmer for 10–15 minutes until the chicken is completely cooked. Adjust the seasoning, if necessary.

4. Divide the rice between four bowls, spoon over the chilli and sprinkle with parsley. Serve immediately with soured cream on the side, if using.

THAI CHICKEN CAKES

SERVES: 4   **PREP TIME: 10 MINS**   **COOK TIME: APPROX. 20 MINS**

INGREDIENTS

½ bunch spring onions, trimmed and roughly chopped

3-cm/1¼-inch piece fresh ginger, roughly chopped

3 garlic cloves, crushed

handful fresh coriander, including the stalks

1 red chilli, deseeded and roughly chopped

500 g/1 lb 2 oz fresh chicken mince

2 tbsp light soy sauce

dash of nam pla (Thai fish sauce)

1 egg white

2 tbsp plain flour

finely grated zest of 1 lime

2–3 tbsp vegetable oil, for frying

pepper

lime wedges and sweet chilli sauce, to serve

1. Place the spring onions, ginger, garlic, coriander and chilli in a food processor or blender and process until everything is finely chopped.

2. Tip into a mixing bowl, add the chicken and combine together with the soy sauce, nam pla, egg white, flour, lime zest and black pepper to taste.

3. Heat a little oil in a non-stick frying pan and add spoonfuls of the mixture in batches. Cook each batch for about 4 minutes on each side, until golden and cooked through. Transfer to a plate and keep warm while cooking the remaining mixture.

4. Serve the cooked Thai chicken cakes with lime wedges and sweet chilli sauce for dipping.

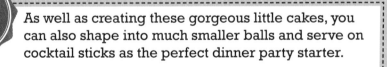

HERO TIPS

As well as creating these gorgeous little cakes, you can also shape into much smaller balls and serve on cocktail sticks as the perfect dinner party starter.

MOROCCAN-STYLE MINCE

SERVES: 4   **PREP TIME: 5 MINS**   **COOK TIME:**
APPROX. 30 MINS

INGREDIENTS

2 tbsp vegetable oil
1 large onion, finely chopped
2 garlic cloves, finely chopped
1 tbsp ground cumin
1 tsp ground cinnamon
2 tsp ground turmeric
500 g/1 lb 2 oz fresh
chicken mince
500 ml/18 fl oz chicken stock
70 g/2½ oz raisins
250 g/9 oz couscous
finely grated zest and juice
of 1 lemon
30 g/1 oz toasted pine kernels
salt and pepper
sprigs of fresh flat-leaf parsley,
to garnish

1. Heat the oil in a large, non-stick frying pan, add the onion and cook over a low heat, stirring occasionally, for 4–5 minutes, until softened. Add the garlic and spices and cook for a further 1 minute over a medium heat.

2. Add the mince and cook, stirring frequently and breaking up the meat with a wooden spoon, for 4–5 minutes, until lightly browned. Add the stock and raisins, cover and cook over a low heat for a further 8–10 minutes.

3. Add the couscous, and salt and pepper to taste, stir and cover again. Simmer for 5–6 minutes, until the couscous has absorbed the stock and is fully cooked.

4. Remove from the heat, then stir in the lemon zest and juice and pine kernels. Garnish with parsley and serve immediately.

SPICY TURKEY SLOPPY JOES

MAKES: 4 **PREP TIME: 10 MINS** **COOK TIME: 25–30 MINS**

INGREDIENTS

1½ tbsp sunflower oil

1 celery stick, finely chopped

1 onion, finely chopped

1 red pepper, deseeded and finely chopped

450 g/1 lb fresh turkey mince

1 tbsp plain flour

½ tsp cayenne pepper, or to taste

1 tsp mixed spice

1 tbsp dried parsley

400 ml/14 fl oz canned cream of tomato soup

125 ml/4 fl oz water

4 tbsp tomato ketchup

1 tbsp Worcestershire sauce

salt and pepper

4 hamburger buns and potato crisps (optional), to serve

1. Heat the oil in a saucepan over a medium–high heat. Add the celery, onion and red pepper and fry, stirring, for 3–5 minutes until soft. Add the turkey and continue frying, stirring with a wooden spoon to break up the meat, for 2–3 minutes, or until the meat loses its raw appearance.

2. Sprinkle in the flour, cayenne pepper, mixed spice and parsley and continue stirring for a further minute.

3. Add the soup, water, ketchup and Worcestershire sauce and season to taste with salt and pepper. Add very little salt because the Worcestershire sauce is salty. Bring to the boil, stirring.

4. Reduce the heat to low and simmer, stirring occasionally, for 12–15 minutes until the turkey is cooked through and the mixture is thickened, taking care that the mixture doesn't stick to the base of the pan. Adjust the seasoning, if necessary.

5. Divide the mixture between the hamburger buns and serve hot with crisps on the side, if using.

CREOLE TURKEY-STUFFED PEPPERS

MAKES: 4 **PREP TIME: 15 MINS** **COOK TIME: 50–55 MINS**

INGREDIENTS

4 large red peppers, about 200 g/7 oz each

1 tbsp sunflower oil, plus extra for greasing

40 g/1½ oz chorizo sausage, skinned and diced

300 g/10½ oz fresh turkey mince

1 celery stick, finely chopped

1 onion, finely chopped

1 small green pepper, deseeded and finely chopped

100 g/3½ oz long-grain easy-cook rice

200 ml/7 fl oz hot chicken stock or vegetable stock

4 tbsp passata

2 tbsp chopped fresh parsley or snipped chives

½ tsp hot pepper sauce, plus extra to serve

salt and pepper

salad leaves, to serve

1. Preheat the oven to 220°C/425°F/Gas Mark 7 and grease a baking dish. Cut off the red pepper tops and remove the cores and seeds, then set the peppers and tops aside.

2. Heat the oil in a frying pan over a medium–high heat. Add the chorizo and fry for 1–2 minutes until it gives off its oil. Transfer to a dish using a slotted spoon and set aside.

3. Pour off all but 2 tablespoons of oil from the pan. Add the turkey, celery, onion and green pepper and fry, stirring with a wooden spoon to break up the turkey into large clumps, for 3–5 minutes until the onion is soft. Stir in the rice.

4. Add the stock, passata, parsley, hot pepper sauce, and salt and pepper to taste. Bring to the boil, stirring. Divide the mixture between the red peppers, then arrange them in the prepared dish, topped with their 'lids'. Carefully pour in boiling water to fill the dish up to 2.5 cm/1 inch, then cover tightly with foil.

5. Bake in the preheated oven for 40–45 minutes, or until the peppers are tender. Serve hot or at room temperature, with salad leaves and the chorizo.

CHILLI CON CARNE

This well-loved favourite is perfect for serving to friends for a causal dinner party. Although it is often accompanied with rice, it is just as delicious with tortilla chips or fresh crusty bread.

SERVES: 6

PREP TIME: 5 MINS

COOK TIME: 1 HR 45 MINS

INGREDIENTS

2 tbsp corn oil

2 onions, thinly sliced

2 garlic cloves, finely chopped

650 g/1 lb 7 oz fresh beef mince

200 g/7 oz canned chopped tomatoes

5 tbsp tomato purée

1 tsp ground cumin

1 tsp cayenne pepper

1 tbsp chilli powder

1 tsp dried oregano

1 bay leaf

350 ml/12 fl oz beef stock

400 g/14 oz canned red kidney beans, drained and rinsed

salt

cooked rice, to serve

1. Heat the oil in a large saucepan. Add the onions and garlic and cook over a low heat, stirring occasionally, for 5 minutes, until softened. Add the beef, increase the heat to medium and cook, stirring frequently and breaking it up with a wooden spoon, for 8–10 minutes, until evenly browned.

2. Stir in the tomatoes, tomato purée, cumin, cayenne pepper, chilli powder, oregano, bay leaf and stock, then season to taste with salt and bring to the boil. Reduce the heat, cover and simmer, stirring occasionally, for 1 hour.

3. Add the kidney beans, re-cover the pan and simmer, stirring occasionally, for a further 30 minutes. Remove and discard the bay leaf and serve immediately with rice.

BEEF & NOODLES

SERVES: 6   **PREP TIME: 10 MINS**   **COOK TIME: 15-20 MINS**

INGREDIENTS

450 g/1 lb dried egg noodles
2 tbsp toasted sesame oil
2 tbsp groundnut oil
1 onion, finely chopped
650 g/1 lb 7 oz fresh beef mince
2.5-cm/1-inch piece fresh
ginger, thinly sliced
1 fresh red chilli, deseeded and
thinly sliced
1½ tsp five-spice powder
2 carrots, thinly sliced
diagonally
1 red pepper, deseeded and
diced
85 g/3 oz mangetout
175 g/6 oz fresh beansprouts

1. Cook the noodles in a saucepan of boiling water for 3-4 minutes, or cook according to the packet instructions, until tender. Tip the noodles into a bowl, add 1 tablespoon of the toasted sesame oil and toss to coat.

2. Heat a wok over a medium heat, then add the groundnut oil, swirl it around the wok and heat. Add the onion and stir-fry for a few minutes, until softened. Add the beef and stir-fry, breaking it up with a wooden spoon, for 3-5 minutes, until evenly browned.

3. Stir in the ginger, chilli and five-spice powder and cook, stirring constantly, for 1 minute, then add the carrots, red pepper and mangetout. Stir-fry for a further 4 minutes.

4. Add the beansprouts, the remaining sesame oil and the noodles and stir-fry for a further 2 minutes. Serve immediately.

2

3

BEEF NACHOS

This quick and easy nacho dip is fabulously fiery and ideal for serving at parties, accompanied with a selection of mouthwatering toppings and tortilla chips for loading.

SERVES: 4–6   **PREP TIME: 10 MINS**   **COOK TIME: 20 MINS**

INGREDIENTS

1 tbsp extra virgin olive oil
450 g/1 lb fresh beef mince
1 tbsp smoked paprika
115 g/4 oz frozen corn kernels
chipotle tomato sauce
115 g/4 oz fresh chopped coriander
salt
tortilla chips, to serve

SUGGESTED TOPPINGS

grated Cheddar cheese
soured cream
hot pepper sauce
shredded lettuce

1. In a large frying pan, heat the oil over medium–high heat. Add the beef and sauté until browned, breaking it up with a wooden spoon, for about 5 minutes. Add the paprika and stir until evenly distributed and aromatic. Add the corn kernels and chipotle tomato sauce.

2. Bring to a simmer, then reduce the heat, partially cover the pan, and simmer, stirring occasionally, for about 10 minutes, or until the beef is cooked through. Season with salt to taste. Stir in the coriander and spoon into bowls. Have your toppings ready and pass them around. Serve the dip immediately with tortilla chips and a selection of toppings.

HERO TIPS

Chipotle sauces are now available in the supermarkets but if you do fail to find a suitable one then search online where you'll find many spicy and delicious variations.

BEEF MEATBALLS WITH SICHUAN CHILLI SAUCE

SERVES: 4

PREP TIME: 20 MINS PLUS CHILLING

COOK TIME: 15 MINS

INGREDIENTS

400 g/14 oz fresh beef mince

½ tbsp grated onion

2-cm/¾-inch piece fresh ginger, squeezed in a garlic press

1 garlic clove, crushed

finely grated zest of ½ lemon

½ tsp salt

¼ tsp pepper

good pinch of chilli flakes

½ beaten egg

2 tsp toasted sesame oil

groundnut oil, for frying

250 ml/9 fl oz ready-made Sichuan sweet chilli sauce

squeeze of lemon juice

3 spring onions, green parts included, shredded

1. Put the meat, onion, ginger, garlic and lemon zest into a bowl and mix well with a fork. Add the salt, pepper and chilli flakes, then stir in the beaten egg and the sesame oil and mix well.

2. Divide the mixture into 20 walnut-sized balls, rolling them in the palm of your hand until firm. Arrange on a plate, cover with clingfilm and chill for 30 minutes, or until you are ready to cook.

3. Add groundnut oil to a wok to a depth of 1 cm/½ inch. Heat to 180°C/350°F, or until a cube of bread browns in 30 seconds.

4. Add the meatballs and fry for 8–10 minutes, turning occasionally with tongs until brown and crusty. Remove from the wok and drain on kitchen paper. Transfer to a warmed serving dish and keep warm.

5. Pour the chilli sauce into a small saucepan and simmer for 2–3 minutes. Add the lemon juice. Pour the sauce over the beef meatballs, scatter over the spring onions and serve immediately.

FRESHNESS FIRST!

Fresh minced red meat, such as beef mince, should have a typical fresh meat smell and an even pink or bright or darker red colour (the depth of the pink/red colour will depend on the type of mince). If the mince looks discoloured (with a brown-grey, grey or dark brown colour all the way through), if it feels tacky, sticky or slimy, or if it has an 'off' or sour odour, then it is very likely to be spoiled, so throw it away. If you are in any doubt about the freshness of the mince (be it minced red meat or minced chicken or turkey), then discard it as it could contain harmful bacteria and may be dangerous to consume.

Darker, evenly coloured minced red meat usually has a lower fat content than minced red meat that is paler in colour or visibly streaked or flecked with white fat. The redder the minced meat, the less visible fat you will see. Choose minced red meat with a low or lower percentage of fat if you can (depending on the recipe you are preparing), and check the label for details of the typical fat content if you are buying from a supermarket or similar outlet. Minced pork and lamb can be fatty, so drain off the excess fat when cooking, or look out for lean minced pork, if you prefer.

For some minced meat recipes though, the mince needs to include a certain amount of fat to give it moisture and flavour as it cooks. For example, choose beef mince that has a higher fat content when making

recipes such as burgers, as the fat will baste and flavour the burgers during cooking, keeping them succulent (some of the fat will also drain away). Select lower-fat beef mince for recipes such as chilli con carne and spaghetti bolognese.

The best place to buy minced meat is from a trusted supplier. Most good butchers will also be happy to mince fresh meat to order, so this enables you to choose a piece of meat and have it minced for you. Free-range or organic mince, including beef, lamb, pork and turkey mince, are also obtainable, although they are likely to be more costly than standard minced meats.

PORK MEATBALLS IN A CHILLI BROTH

SERVES: 4

PREP TIME: 20 MINS PLUS CHILLING

COOK TIME: 25 MINS

INGREDIENTS

1.2 litres/2 pints chicken stock

¼–½ fresh red chilli, deseeded and very finely sliced

½ tsp palm sugar or soft light brown sugar

3 fresh thyme sprigs

2 lemon grass stalks, fibrous outer leaves removed, stems bashed with the flat of a knife

¼ tsp pepper

1 small head pak choi, stems cut into small squares, leaves sliced into ribbons

1 spring onion, green parts included, sliced diagonally

dash of soy sauce

salt and pepper

PORK MEATBALLS

225 g/8 oz fresh pork mince

1 shallot, grated

2-cm/¾-inch piece fresh ginger, crushed

1 garlic clove, crushed

finely grated zest and juice of ½ lime

6 tbsp groundnut oil

1. Pour the stock into a medium-sized saucepan. Add the chilli, sugar, thyme, lemon grass, pepper, and salt to taste and bring to the boil. Reduce the heat and simmer gently for 10 minutes. Remove from the heat and leave to cool for about 30 minutes.

2. To make the meatballs, combine the pork, shallot, ginger, garlic, lime zest and juice and season. Mix well with a fork. Line a plate with kitchen paper.

3. Divide the mixture into 16–20 walnut-sized balls. Place on the prepared plate and chill for 30 minutes.

4. Heat a large wok over a high heat. Add the oil and heat until very hot. Add the pork meatballs and fry for 5–6 minutes, until golden brown all over and cooked through. Drain on kitchen paper and keep warm.

5. Remove the thyme and lemon grass from the broth. Add the pak choi and spring onion. Bring to the boil then simmer for 2 minutes until the pak choi stalks are just tender. Season with soy sauce.

6. Ladle the broth and vegetables over the meatballs and serve immediately.

ANTS CLIMBING A TREE

This oddly named Chinese dish comes from the effect of the tiny pieces of minced meat clinging to the noodles, which look like ants climbing on twigs!

SERVES: 4

PREP TIME: 10 MINS PLUS MARINATING

COOK TIME: 6 MINS

INGREDIENTS

250 g/9 oz thick rice noodles

1 tbsp cornflour

3 tbsp soy sauce

1½ tbsp Chinese rice wine

1½ tsp sugar

1½ tsp sesame oil

350 g/12 oz fresh lean beef mince

1½ tbsp groundnut oil

2 large garlic cloves, finely chopped

1 large fresh red chilli, or to taste, deseeded and thinly sliced

3 spring onions, finely chopped

finely chopped fresh coriander, to garnish

1. Cook the noodles according to the packet instructions, drain well and set aside.

2. Meanwhile, put the cornflour in a separate large bowl, then stir in the soy sauce, rice wine, sugar and sesame oil, stirring until smooth. Add the mince and use your hands to toss the ingredients together without squeezing the beef. Set aside to marinate for 10 minutes.

3. Heat a wok over a high heat, then add the groundnut oil. Add the garlic, chilli and spring onions and stir around for about 30 seconds. Tip in the mince together with any marinade left in the bowl and stir-fry for about 5 minutes, or until the beef is no longer pink. Add the noodles and use 2 forks to mix together. Sprinkle with the chopped coriander and serve.

BEEF & LAMB KOFTAS

MAKES: 4

PREP TIME: 15 MINS PLUS CHILLING

COOK TIME: 10 MINS

INGREDIENTS

200 g/7 oz fresh beef mince

100 g/3½ oz fresh lamb mince

½ onion, grated

2 tbsp chopped fresh flat-leaf parsley

1 tbsp chopped fresh coriander

1 garlic clove, very finely chopped

1 tsp ground cumin

¼ tsp ground cinnamon

½ tsp hot paprika, or to taste

½ tsp harissa paste, or to taste

½ tsp salt

pinch of cayenne pepper, or to taste

olive oil, for brushing

mixed salad and warmed pitta bread, to serve

1. Put the beef and lamb mince in a food processor and process to a paste. Add the onion, herbs, garlic, cumin, cinnamon, paprika, harissa paste, salt and cayenne pepper and process again until blended.

2. Divide the mixture into 4. Wrap the mixture around metal skewers to form oval shapes. Cover with clingfilm and chill in the refrigerator for at least 1 hour, but ideally up to 4 hours.

3. Preheat the grill. Brush the meatballs with a little oil and cook under the preheated grill for 10 minutes, turning frequently, and brushing with more oil if necessary, until cooked through.

4. Using a folded cloth to protect your fingers, hold the top of each skewer and use a fork to push the meatballs off. Serve with a mixed salad and warmed pitta bread.

CHILLI LAMB

This spicy lamb dish is certainly one for ringing the changes. Vary the fresh chilli and chilli powder according to taste and serve with naan bread for scooping up every last tasty morsel.

SERVES: 6　　　　　**PREP TIME: 15 MINS**　　　　**COOK TIME: 25–30 MINS**

INGREDIENTS

2 tbsp sunflower oil

1 onion, chopped

1 garlic clove, finely chopped

1 tsp grated fresh ginger

1 tsp ground coriander

½ tsp chilli powder

¼ tsp ground turmeric

pinch of salt

350 g/12 oz fresh lean lamb mince

200 g/7 oz canned chopped tomatoes

1 tbsp chopped fresh mint

85 g/3 oz fresh or frozen peas

2 carrots, sliced into thin batons

1 fresh green chilli, deseeded and finely chopped

1 tbsp chopped fresh coriander

naan bread, to serve

1. Heat the oil in a large, heavy-based frying pan or flameproof casserole. Add the onion and cook over a low heat, stirring occasionally, for 10 minutes, or until golden.

2. Meanwhile, place the garlic, ginger, ground coriander, chilli powder, turmeric and salt in a small bowl and mix well. Add the spice mixture to the pan and cook, stirring constantly, for 2 minutes. Add the lamb and cook, stirring frequently and breaking up the lamb with a wooden spoon, for 8–10 minutes, or until browned all over.

3. Add the tomatoes, chopped mint, peas, carrots, chilli and chopped coriander. Cook, stirring constantly, for 3–5 minutes. Serve immediately with naan bread.

PASTA PARTNERS

CHICKEN MEATBALL PASTA

Chicken meatballs provide a much lighter and more delicately flavoured alternative to the classic beef variety. They are still just as delicious though and every bit as filling.

SERVES: 4   **PREP TIME: 15 MINS**   **COOK TIME: 35 MINS**

INGREDIENTS

3 tbsp olive oil

1 red onion, chopped

400 g/14 oz skinless, boneless chicken breasts, chopped

55 g/2 oz fresh white breadcrumbs

2 tsp dried oregano

1 garlic clove, crushed

400 g/14 oz canned chopped tomatoes

1 tbsp sun-dried tomato paste

300 ml/10 fl oz water

225 g/8 oz dried spaghetti or linguine

salt and pepper

Parmesan cheese shavings, to serve

1. Heat 1 tablespoon of the oil in a large frying pan and fry half the chopped onion for 5 minutes, until just softened. Leave to cool.

2. Place the chicken, breadcrumbs, oregano and the fried onion in a food processor or blender. Season to taste well with salt and pepper, and process for 2–3 minutes, until thoroughly combined. Shape into 24 meatballs.

3. Heat the remaining oil in the frying pan and fry the meatballs over a medium–high heat for 3–4 minutes, until golden brown. Remove and set aside.

4. Add the remaining onion and the garlic to the pan and fry for 5 minutes. Stir in the tomatoes, sun-dried tomato paste and water, and bring to the boil. Add the meatballs and simmer for 20 minutes. Season to taste with salt and pepper.

5. Meanwhile, bring a large saucepan of lightly salted water to the boil. Add the pasta, bring back to the boil and cook for 8–10 minutes, until tender but still firm to the bite. Drain thoroughly and toss with the meatballs and sauce. Serve immediately with Parmesan cheese shavings.

CHICKEN & MUSHROOM LASAGNE

SERVES: 4-6   **PREP TIME: 15 MINS**   **COOK TIME: 1½ HRS**

INGREDIENTS

2 tbsp olive oil

1 large onion, finely chopped

500 g/1 lb 2 oz fresh chicken or turkey mince

100 g/3½ oz smoked pancetta, chopped

250 g/9 oz chestnut mushrooms, chopped

100 g/3½ oz dried porcini mushrooms, soaked

150 ml/5 fl oz dry white wine

400 g/14 oz canned chopped tomatoes

3 tbsp chopped fresh basil leaves

9 dried no pre-cook lasagne sheets

3 tbsp finely grated Parmesan cheese

salt and pepper

BÉCHAMEL SAUCE

600 ml/1 pint milk

55 g/2 oz butter

55 g/2 oz plain flour

1 bay leaf

1. Preheat the oven to 190°C/375°F/Gas Mark 5. For the sauce, heat the milk, butter, flour and bay leaf in a saucepan, whisking constantly, until smooth and thick. Season to taste with salt and pepper, cover and leave to stand.

2. Heat the oil in a large saucepan and fry the onion, stirring, for 3–4 minutes. Add the chicken and pancetta and cook for 6–8 minutes. Stir in both types of mushrooms and cook for a further 2–3 minutes.

3. Add the wine and bring to the boil. Pour in the tomatoes, cover and simmer for 20 minutes. Stir in the basil.

4. Arrange three of the lasagne sheets in a rectangular ovenproof dish, then spoon over a third of the meat sauce. Remove and discard the bay leaf from the white sauce. Spread a third of the sauce over the meat. Repeat the layers twice more, finishing with a layer of Béchamel Sauce.

5. Sprinkle with the cheese and bake in the preheated oven for 35–40 minutes, until the topping is golden and bubbling. Serve immediately.

CHICKEN & ORZO BAKE

SERVES: 4 **PREP TIME: 15 MINS** **COOK TIME: 40 MINS**

INGREDIENTS

100 g/3½ oz ricotta cheese, drained

125 g/4½ oz mozzarella cheese, drained and grated

55 g/2 oz Gruyère cheese, finely grated

125 g/4½ oz dried orzo pasta

2 tbsp olive oil, plus extra for oiling and drizzling

1 large onion, finely chopped

450 g/1 lb fresh chicken mince

4 large garlic cloves, finely chopped

1 tbsp dried mixed herbs

500 ml/18 fl oz passata

40 g/1½ oz fine dried breadcrumbs

salt and pepper

1. Preheat the oven to 220°C/425°F/Gas Mark 7 and oil a 1.2-litre/2-pint ovenproof serving dish. Beat together the ricotta cheese, mozzarella cheese and half the Gruyère cheese in a large bowl and set aside.

2. Bring a saucepan of lightly salted water to the boil. Add the pasta, bring back to the boil and cook for 2 minutes less than specified in the packet instructions.

3. Meanwhile, heat the oil in a frying pan over a medium–high heat. Add the onion and fry, stirring, for 2–3 minutes until soft. Add the chicken, garlic and herbs, stirring with a wooden spoon to break up the chicken into large clumps, for about 2 minutes until it loses its raw appearance. Stir in the passata, season to taste with salt and pepper, bring to the boil, then simmer for 10 minutes.

4. Drain the pasta and immediately tip it into the bowl with the cheese. Add the chicken mixture, stirring until the cheeses melt.

5. Pour into the prepared dish and smooth the surface. Combine the remaining Gruyère cheese with the breadcrumbs and sprinkle over the top, then drizzle with oil. Bake in the preheated oven for 20–25 minutes until the top is golden brown and bubbling. Serve immediately.

TURKEY & MUSHROOM CANNELLONI

SERVES: 4   **PREP TIME: 15 MINS**   **COOK TIME: 1¾ HRS**

INGREDIENTS

butter, for greasing
2 tbsp olive oil
2 garlic cloves, crushed
1 large onion, finely chopped
225 g/8 oz wild mushrooms, sliced
350 g/12 oz fresh turkey mince
115 g/4 oz prosciutto, diced
150 ml/5 fl oz Marsala
200 g/7 oz canned chopped tomatoes
1 tbsp shredded fresh basil leaves
2 tbsp tomato purée
10–12 dried cannelloni tubes
600 ml/1 pint Béchamel Sauce (see page 74)
85 g/3 oz freshly grated Parmesan cheese
salt and pepper

1. Preheat the oven to 190°C/375°F/Gas Mark 5. Lightly grease a large ovenproof dish. Heat the oil in a heavy-based frying pan. Add the garlic, onion and mushrooms and cook over a low heat, stirring frequently, for 8–10 minutes. Add the turkey mince and prosciutto and cook, stirring frequently, for 12 minutes, or until browned all over. Stir in the Marsala, tomatoes, basil and tomato purée and cook for 4 minutes. Season to taste with salt and pepper, then cover and simmer for 30 minutes. Uncover, stir and simmer for 15 minutes.

2. Meanwhile, bring a large saucepan of lightly salted water to the boil. Add the cannelloni tubes, bring back to the boil and cook for 8–10 minutes, until tender but still firm to the bite. Using a slotted spoon, transfer the cannelloni tubes to a plate and pat dry with kitchen paper.

3. Using a teaspoon, fill the cannelloni tubes with the turkey and mushroom mixture. Transfer them to the dish. Pour the Béchamel Sauce over them to cover completely and sprinkle with the grated Parmesan cheese.

4. Bake in the preheated oven for 30 minutes, or until golden and bubbling. Serve immediately.

TURKEY PASTA PESTO

All along the Italian Liguria coast trattorias serve the regional speciality of thin, long pasta shapes called *trofie*, boiled new potatoes and French beans, all tossed together with home-made pesto sauce. Here, turkey mince makes this a more substantial main course.

SERVES: 4   **PREP TIME: 10 MINS**   **COOK TIME: 12 MINS**

INGREDIENTS

150 g/5½ oz dried trofie pasta or thin penne pasta

100 g/3½ oz new potatoes, scrubbed and thinly sliced

100 g/3½ oz fine French beans, topped and tailed and cut about the same length as the pasta

2 tbsp olive oil

450 g/1 lb fresh turkey mince

2 large garlic cloves, crushed

150 g/5½ oz pesto sauce

salt and pepper

freshly grated Parmesan cheese or pecorino cheese, to serve

1. Bring a large saucepan of water to the boil with 1 teaspoon of salt. Add the pasta, bring back to the boil and cook for 12 minutes, or according to the packet instructions. Add the potatoes 7 minutes before the end of the cooking time, then add the beans 2 minutes later.

2. Meanwhile, heat the oil in a large frying pan over a medium–high heat. Add the turkey and fry, stirring with a wooden spoon to break it up into large clumps, for about 5 minutes until just starting to brown. Add the garlic and fry for a further minute, or until the turkey is cooked through. Remove from the pan and keep hot.

3. When the pasta and vegetables are tender, drain, reserving a few tablespoons of the cooking water. Return the pasta and vegetables to the pan, add the turkey and pesto and toss together well. Add a little of the reserved cooking water, if necessary. Season to taste with salt and pepper.

4. Divide the mixture between warmed bowls and serve immediately, with plenty of cheese for sprinkling over.

2

3

3

TURKEY STROGANOFF

SERVES: 4 **PREP TIME: 10 MINS** **COOK TIME: 25 MINS**

INGREDIENTS

3 tbsp sunflower oil

450 g/1 lb fresh turkey mince

30 g/1 oz butter

1 onion, very finely chopped

2 large garlic cloves, very finely chopped

250 g/9 oz chestnut mushrooms, trimmed and thinly chopped

4 tsp Dijon mustard

freshly grated nutmeg, to taste

450 ml/16 fl oz soured cream

freshly squeezed lemon juice, to taste

salt and pepper

finely chopped fresh flat-leaf parsley and cooked tagliatelle, to serve

1. Heat the oil in a large frying pan over a medium–high heat. Add the turkey and fry, stirring with a wooden spoon to break up the meat into large clumps, for 4–6 minutes until cooked through. Remove from the pan with a slotted spoon and set aside.

2. Pour off all but 1 tablespoon of the fat remaining in the pan. Add the butter and heat until melted. Add the onion and fry, stirring, for 3–5 minutes until soft. Stir in the garlic and mushrooms and season to taste with salt and pepper. Fry, stirring, for about 5 minutes until the mushrooms re-absorb the liquid they give off.

3. Stir in the mustard and nutmeg, then return the turkey to the pan. Stir in the soured cream and bring to the boil, stirring. Reduce the heat and simmer for a few minutes until slightly reduced. Add lemon juice to taste and adjust the seasoning, if necessary.

4. Divide the pasta between four plates and pour over the sauce. Sprinkle with parsley and serve immediately.

BOLOGNESE SAUCE

SERVES: 4

PREP TIME: 10 MINS PLUS SOAKING

COOK TIME: 1¼ HRS

INGREDIENTS

25 g/1 oz dried ceps
125 ml/4 fl oz lukewarm water
1 tbsp butter
55 g/2 oz pancetta, diced
1 small onion, finely chopped
1 garlic clove, finely chopped
2 small carrots, finely diced
2 celery sticks, finely diced
300 g/10½ oz beef mince
1 pinch sugar
freshly grated nutmeg
1 tbsp tomato purée
125 ml/4 fl oz red wine
250 ml/9 fl oz passata
salt and pepper

1. Soak the ceps in the water for 20 minutes.

2. Melt the butter in a saucepan, add the pancetta and fry.

3. Add the onion and garlic and fry until the onion is translucent. Stir in the carrots and celery and cook for a few minutes, stirring frequently.

4. Add the beef and fry, stirring constantly. Season with salt and pepper, the sugar and some nutmeg. Stir in the tomato purée and cook for a minute or two, then add the wine. Mix in the passata. Thinly slice the ceps and add them to the sauce. Pour the soaking water through a fine sieve into the sauce. Thicken the sauce by cooking it over a low heat for 1 hour.

HERO TIPS

Spaghetti is the obvious partner to go with this rich Bolognese sauce but any pasta would be equally delicious. Alternatively, simply serve with rice or fresh crusty bread.

SPAGHETTI & MEATBALLS

This famous Italian-American dish is a favourite with both adults and children alike. This version uses smaller meatballs but you can have fewer – but much larger – meatballs if you prefer.

SERVES: 4   **PREP TIME: 25 MINS**   **COOK TIME: 35 MINS**

INGREDIENTS

1 tbsp olive oil
1 small onion, finely chopped
2 garlic cloves, finely chopped
2 fresh thyme sprigs, finely chopped
650 g/1 lb 7 oz fresh beef mince
25 g/1 oz fresh breadcrumbs
1 egg, lightly beaten
450 g/1 lb dried spaghetti
salt and pepper

SAUCE

1 onion, cut into wedges
3 red peppers, halved and deseeded
400 g/14 oz canned chopped tomatoes
1 bay leaf
salt and pepper

1. Heat the oil in a frying pan. Add the chopped onion and garlic and cook over a low heat, for 5 minutes, until softened. Remove from the heat and tip the mixture into a bowl with the thyme, beef, breadcrumbs and egg. Season to taste with salt and pepper and mix well. Shape into 20 meatballs.

2. Heat a large non-stick frying pan over a low–medium heat. Add the meatballs and cook, stirring gently and turning frequently, for 15 minutes, until lightly browned all over.

3. Meanwhile, preheat the grill. Put the onion wedges and pepper halves, skin-side up, on a grill rack and cook under the preheated grill, turning frequently, for 10 minutes, until the pepper skins are blistered and charred. Put the peppers into a plastic bag, tie the top and leave to cool. Set the onion wedges aside.

4. Peel off the pepper skins. Roughly chop the flesh and put it into a food processor or blender with the onion wedges and tomatoes. Process to a smooth

purée and season to taste with salt and pepper. Pour into a saucepan with the bay leaf and bring to the boil. Reduce the heat and simmer, stirring occasionally, for 10 minutes. Remove and discard the bay leaf.

5. Meanwhile, bring a saucepan of salted water to the boil. Add the spaghetti, return to the boil and cook for 8–10 minutes, until tender but still firm to the bite. Drain the spaghetti and serve immediately with the meatballs and sauce.

AMERICAN-STYLE LASAGNE

Many countries have their own version of this Italian classic. This American-style lasagne omits any white sauce but instead opts for layers of Parmesan cheese before the whole dish is smothered with chopped tomatoes.

SERVES: 4   **PREP TIME: 15 MINS**   **COOK TIME: 1¾ HRS PLUS STANDING**

INGREDIENTS

2 tbsp olive oil
55 g/2 oz pancetta or bacon, chopped
1 garlic clove, finely chopped
1 onion, chopped
225 g/8 oz fresh beef mince
2 carrots, chopped
2 celery sticks, chopped
115 g/4 oz mushrooms, chopped
pinch of dried oregano
5 tbsp red wine
150 ml/5 fl oz beef stock
1 tbsp sun-dried tomato paste
225 g/8 oz dried no pre-cook lasagne sheets
115 g/4 oz Parmesan cheese, grated
400 g/14 oz canned chopped tomatoes
few fresh basil leaves, torn
salt and pepper
mixed salad, to serve

1. Heat the oil in a large saucepan. Add the pancetta and cook over a medium heat, stirring occasionally, for 2–3 minutes. Reduce the heat to low, add the garlic and onion and cook, stirring occasionally, for 5 minutes, until softened.

2. Add the beef, increase the heat to medium and cook, stirring frequently and breaking it up with a wooden spoon, for 8–10 minutes, until evenly browned. Stir in the carrots, celery and mushrooms and cook, stirring occasionally, for a further 5 minutes. Add the oregano, pour in the wine and stock and stir in the sun-dried tomato paste. Season to taste with salt and pepper. Bring to the boil, reduce the heat and simmer for 40 minutes.

3. Preheat the oven to 190°C/375°F/Gas Mark 5. Make alternating layers of the beef sauce, lasagne sheets and Parmesan in a large, rectangular ovenproof dish. Pour the tomatoes over the top to cover completely. Bake in the preheated oven for 30 minutes. Remove the dish from the oven and leave to stand for 10 minutes, then sprinkle with torn basil, cut into four and serve with a mixed salad.

MEATY MACARONI CHEESE

Give this student staple a twist by adding beef mince to create a hearty, filling meal. After trying this tasty remix, you may even be reluctant to go back to the classic meat-free version!

SERVES: 4   **PREP TIME: 15 MINS**   **COOK TIME: 1 HR 15 MINS**

INGREDIENTS

2 tbsp olive oil
1 onion, chopped
1 garlic clove, finely chopped
500 g/1 lb 2 oz fresh beef mince
200 g/7 oz canned sweetcorn, drained
400 g/14 oz canned chopped tomatoes
1 tsp dried mixed herbs
225 g/8 oz dried macaroni
40 g/1½ oz butter
40 g/1½ oz plain flour
500 ml/18 fl oz milk
2 tsp Dijon mustard
200 g/7 oz Cheddar cheese, grated
salt and pepper

1. Heat the oil in a saucepan. Add the onion and garlic and cook over a low heat, stirring occasionally, for 5 minutes, until softened. Add the beef, increase the heat to medium and cook, breaking it up with a wooden spoon, for 8–10 minutes, until lightly browned all over. Stir in the sweetcorn, tomatoes and mixed herbs and season to taste with salt and pepper. Reduce the heat, cover and simmer, stirring occasionally, for 25–30 minutes.

2. Bring a large pan of salted water to the boil. Add the macaroni, return to the boil and cook for 10 minutes, until tender but still firm to the bite.

3. Meanwhile, preheat the grill. Melt the butter in a separate saucepan. Sprinkle in the flour and cook, stirring constantly, for 2 minutes. Remove the pan from the heat and gradually stir in the milk, a little at a time. Return the pan to the heat and bring to the boil, stirring constantly. Reduce the heat and simmer the sauce, stirring constantly, for 5 minutes, until thickened and smooth. Remove the pan from the heat and stir in the mustard and 150 g/5½ oz of the cheese. Stir well until the cheese has melted.

4. Drain the macaroni and tip it into the cheese sauce, stirring well to mix. Spoon the beef mixture into a baking dish, then cover with the macaroni mixture. Sprinkle with the remaining cheese and cook under the preheated grill for 4–5 minutes, until the top is golden and bubbling. Serve immediately.

ONE POT BEEF & PASTA

SERVES: 4   **PREP TIME: 15 MINS**   **COOK TIME: 30–40 MINS**

INGREDIENTS

2 tbsp olive oil
1 onion, chopped
1 garlic clove, finely chopped
1 celery stick, chopped
1 carrot, chopped
500 g/1 lb 2 oz fresh lean beef mince
115 g/4 oz mushrooms, sliced
400 g/14 oz canned chopped tomatoes
1 tbsp tomato purée
1 tsp sugar
pinch of dried oregano
1 tbsp chopped fresh flat-leaf parsley
175 g/6 oz dried fusilli
175 ml/6 fl oz red wine
1½ tbsp concentrated beef stock or 1 beef stock cube
salt and pepper

1. Heat the oil in a large saucepan with a tight-fitting lid. Add the onion, garlic, celery and carrot and cook over a low heat, stirring occasionally, for 5 minutes, until softened. Add the beef, increase the heat to medium and cook, stirring frequently and breaking up the beef with a wooden spoon, for 5–8 minutes, until evenly browned.

2. Add the mushrooms and cook for a further 3–4 minutes. Add the tomatoes, tomato purée, sugar, herbs, pasta and wine. Stir in the concentrated stock, add just enough water to cover and stir well.

3. Reduce the heat, cover tightly and simmer gently for 15–20 minutes, until the pasta is tender but still firm to the bite and the sauce has thickened. Season to taste with salt and pepper. Serve immediately.

STORE YOUR KNOWLEDGE!

Due to the large surface area of minced meat, it tends to have a shorter shelf life than most other fresh meats. Once ground or minced, meat begins to lose quality and flavour, so it should be used quickly and should always be cooked until well done. If you are mincing/grinding your own meat, then ideally mince/grind it just before you plan to use it.

Minced meat should be stored in a covered or airtight container (so that any juices don't drip and contaminate other foods) in the bottom of the refrigerator and should be eaten within 1–2 days, or check the 'use-by' date, if it's provided on the packaging. If you buy mince from a supermarket or similar outlet, you can store the mince in its original packaging (some mince comes in vacuum packs), so long as it is airtight and sealed.

Minced meat should be frozen on the day of purchase and used within 1 month. Frozen mince should be thawed thoroughly in the refrigerator overnight (in a dish to catch any juices) before use. It should then be cooked as soon as possible, within 24 hours. Do not re-freeze thawed minced meat, however, you can freeze it again once it is cooked in recipes.

Chilled fresh mycoprotein mince should be stored in the refrigerator and used by the 'use-by' date. Once opened, it should be kept in a covered or airtight container in the refrigerator and used within 24 hours. Chilled fresh mycoprotein mince can also be frozen on the day of purchase for up to 3 months. As with minced meat, do not re-freeze thawed mycoprotein mince, however, you can freeze it again (for up to 1 month) once it is cooked. Ready-frozen mycoprotein mince can be cooked from frozen or thawed before use, but check the packaging for more guidelines on this.

PORK & PASTA BAKE

SERVES: 4   **PREP TIME: 10 MINS**   **COOK TIME: 1¼ HRS**

INGREDIENTS

2 tbsp olive oil

1 onion, chopped

1 garlic clove, finely chopped

2 carrots, diced

55 g/2 oz pancetta, chopped

115 g/4 oz mushrooms, chopped

450 g/1 lb fresh pork mince

125 ml/4 fl oz dry white wine

4 tbsp passata

200 g/7 oz canned chopped tomatoes

2 tsp chopped fresh sage

225 g/8 oz dried penne

140 g/5 oz mozzarella cheese, diced

4 tbsp freshly grated Parmesan cheese

300 ml/10 fl oz Béchamel Sauce (see page 74)

salt and pepper

1. Preheat the oven to 200°C/400°F/Gas Mark 6. Heat the oil in a large, heavy-based frying pan. Add the onion, garlic and carrots and cook over a low heat, stirring occasionally, for 5 minutes, or until the onion has softened.

2. Add the pancetta and cook for 5 minutes. Add the chopped mushrooms and cook, stirring occasionally, for a further 2 minutes. Add the pork and cook until the meat is browned. Stir in the wine, passata, tomatoes and chopped fresh sage. Season to taste with salt and pepper, bring to the boil, then cover and simmer over a low heat for 25–30 minutes.

3. Meanwhile, bring a large, heavy-based saucepan of lightly salted water to the boil. Add the pasta, return to the boil and cook for 8–10 minutes, or until tender but still firm to the bite. Spoon the pork mixture into a large ovenproof dish. Stir the mozzarella cheese and half the Parmesan cheese into the Béchamel Sauce.

4. Drain the pasta and stir the sauce into it, then spoon it over the pork mixture. Sprinkle with the remaining Parmesan cheese and bake in the preheated oven for 25–30 minutes, or until golden brown. Serve immediately.

PASTICCIO

This recipe shares its origins with a traditional Greek bake made with lamb. It is delicious served hot or cold with a fresh side salad – or vegetables, if you prefer.

SERVES: 4   **PREP TIME: 10 MINS**   **COOK TIME: APPROX. 1 HR 40 MINS**

INGREDIENTS

1 tbsp olive oil
1 onion, chopped
2 garlic cloves, finely chopped
450 g/1 lb fresh lamb mince
2 tbsp tomato purée
2 tbsp plain flour
300 ml/10 fl oz chicken stock
1 tsp ground cinnamon
115 g/4 oz dried macaroni
2 beef tomatoes, sliced
300 ml/10 fl oz Greek yogurt
2 eggs, lightly beaten
salt and pepper
salad leaves, to serve

1. Preheat the oven to 190°C/375°F/Gas Mark 5. Heat the oil in a large, heavy-based frying pan. Add the onion and garlic and cook over a low heat, stirring occasionally, for 5 minutes, or until softened. Add the lamb and cook, breaking it up with a wooden spoon, until browned all over. Add the tomato purée and sprinkle in the flour. Cook, stirring, for 1 minute, then stir in the chicken stock. Season to taste with salt and pepper and stir in the cinnamon. Bring to the boil, reduce the heat, cover and cook for 25 minutes.

2. Meanwhile, bring a large, heavy-based saucepan of lightly salted water to the boil. Add the pasta, return to the boil and cook for 8–10 minutes, or until tender but still firm to the bite.

3. Drain the pasta and stir into the lamb mixture. Spoon into a large ovenproof dish and arrange the tomato slices on top. Beat together the yogurt and eggs then spoon over the lamb evenly. Bake in the preheated oven for 1 hour. Serve immediately with salad leaves.

TASTY APPETIZERS

MINCED CHICKEN SKEWERS

MAKES: 8   **PREP TIME: 10 MINS**   **COOK TIME: 8-10 MINS**

INGREDIENTS

450 g/1 lb fresh chicken mince

1 onion, finely chopped

1 fresh red chilli,
deseeded and chopped

2 tbsp Thai red curry paste

1 tsp palm sugar or soft light
brown sugar

1 tsp ground coriander

1 tsp ground cumin

1 egg white

8 lemon grass stalks

cooked rice with chopped
spring onion, to serve

coriander sprigs, to garnish

1. Mix the chicken, onion, chilli, curry paste and sugar together in a bowl to a thick paste. Stir in the coriander, cumin and egg white and mix again.

2. Preheat the grill to high. Divide the mixture into 8 equal portions and squeeze each one around a lemon grass stalk. Arrange on a grill rack and cook under the preheated grill, turning frequently, for 8 minutes, or until browned and cooked through. Serve immediately, accompanied by cooked rice with chopped spring onion stirred through it. Garnish with the coriander sprigs.

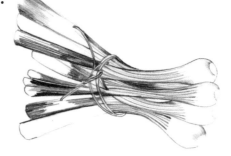

HERO TIPS

You can also serve the skewers with a fresh salad and a dipping sauce. Try mixing dark soy sauce with a few chilli flakes, some minced ginger and garlic and a splash of sesame oil.

DIM SUM

These tasty little Cantonese parcels are traditionally served in small steamer baskets or on small plates and with tea – such as green tea or chrysanthemum tea.

MAKES: 20–24   **PREP TIME: 20 MINS**   **COOK TIME: 15–25 MINS**

INGREDIENTS

300 g/10½ oz fresh chicken mince

½ bunch spring onions, trimmed and very finely chopped

2 tbsp finely chopped fresh coriander

1 tbsp soy sauce

1 tbsp grated fresh ginger

1 tbsp rice wine vinegar

20–24 wonton wrappers

pepper

sweet chilli sauce and dark soy sauce, to serve

1. Put the mince, spring onions, coriander, soy sauce, ginger and vinegar into a bowl and use a fork to combine. Season to taste with pepper.

2. Place a teaspoon of the prepared filling in the centre of each wonton wrapper. Use your fingers to rub the edges of the wrappers with warm water, gather the 2 opposite edges to form a tight seal, then bring together the remaining 2 sides in the middle at the top.

3. Cover the base of a bamboo steamer with a single layer of the dim sum. Alternatively, line the base of a steamer pan with some baking paper and cover with the dim sum. Place over a saucepan of boiling water, cover and steam for 7–8 minutes.

4. Remove from the steam and serve immediately with the chilli sauce and soy sauce for dipping.

MINI CHIMICHANGAS

MAKES: ABOUT 10   PREP TIME: 20–25 MINS   COOK TIME: 25–30 MINS

INGREDIENTS

2 tbsp vegetable oil,
plus extra for frying

1 onion, finely chopped

250 g/9 oz fresh chicken mince

1 red chilli, deseeded and
finely chopped

1 red pepper, deseeded and
very finely chopped

100 g/3½ oz canned sweetcorn,
drained

4 spring onions, trimmed and
finely chopped

4 tbsp fresh tomato salsa

10 small flour tortillas

salt and pepper

1. Heat the 2 tablespoons of the oil in a non-stick frying pan, add the onion and mince and cook for 4–5 minutes, until the chicken starts to change colour and the onion is soft.

2. Add the chilli and red pepper and cook for a further 2–3 minutes. Remove from the heat and stir in the sweetcorn, spring onions, salsa, and salt and pepper to taste and place in a bowl. Wipe out the pan with kitchen paper.

3. Warm a tortilla briefly on each side in the pan. Place a large spoonful of the filling in the centre, fold in 2 sides of the tortilla, then the remaining 2 sides to form a small parcel. Secure with a wooden cocktail stick. Repeat with the remaining tortillas and filling.

HERO TIPS

If using a deep-fat fryer be sure to fry only 2–3 chimichangas at a time as advised. Overcrowding the fryer will cause the oil temperature to drop and result in soggy parcels.

4. Heat enough oil for frying in a frying pan. Add 2–3 chimichangas and cook for 2 minutes, then turn and cook for a further 2–3 minutes, until evenly golden brown. Alternatively, heat enough oil for deep-frying in a deep-fat fryer to 180–190°C/350–375°F, or until a cube of bread browns in 30 seconds. Add 2–3 chimichangas and cook for 2–3 minutes, until golden brown. Drain on kitchen paper and keep warm while cooking the remaining chimichangas. Serve immediately.

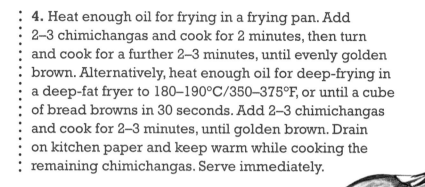

TURKEY & CHORIZO EMPANADAS

MAKES: 8   **PREP TIME: 30 MINS**   **COOK TIME: 30–35 MINS**

INGREDIENTS

2 tbsp vegetable oil, plus extra for greasing

1 onion, finely chopped

2 garlic cloves, finely chopped

250 g/9 oz fresh turkey mince

50 g/1¾ oz chorizo sausage, finely chopped

2 tsp smoked paprika

1 yellow pepper, deseeded and finely chopped

70 g/2½ oz frozen peas

2 tbsp fresh flat-leaf parsley, finely chopped

500 g/1 lb 2 oz ready-made shortcrust pastry

1 small egg, beaten

salt and pepper

1. Preheat the oven to 180°C/350°F/Gas Mark 4. Heat the oil in a non-stick frying pan, add the onion and cook for 4–5 minutes, until softened. Add the garlic and cook for a further 1 minute.

2. Add the mince, chorizo, paprika and yellow pepper and continue to cook for a further 6–8 minutes, until the mince is evenly browned. Stir in the peas, parsley, and salt and pepper to taste.

3. Roll out the pastry on a lightly floured work surface and use a saucer to cut out 8 rounds. Spoon a small amount of the filling onto one half of each round. Use a pastry brush to brush the edges of the pastry with a little beaten egg and fold the rounds in half over the filling, crimping the edges to form a tight seal.

4. Lightly grease a baking tray with oil. Place the empanadas on the prepared tray and brush each one with the remaining beaten egg. Bake in the preheated oven for 15–18 minutes until golden. Serve immediately.

BEEF & PINE NUT TRIANGLES

MAKES: 15   **PREP TIME: 30–40 MINS**   **COOK TIME: 30–35 MINS**

INGREDIENTS

1 tbsp olive oil
1 small onion, chopped
2 garlic cloves, finely chopped
1 tsp ground coriander
1 tsp ground cumin
300 g/10½ oz fresh beef mince
4 tbsp chopped fresh mint
2 tbsp pine nuts
2 potatoes, cut into chunks
55 g/2 oz Kefalotiri or Cheddar cheese, grated
115 g/4 oz butter, melted
10 sheets filo pastry
salt
tomato and basil salsa, to serve

1. Heat the oil in a large frying pan. Add the onion and garlic and cook over a low heat, stirring occasionally, for 5 minutes, until softened. Stir in the coriander and cumin and cook, stirring occasionally, for a further 3 minutes. Add the beef, half the mint and the pine nuts. Increase the heat to medium and cook, stirring and breaking up the meat with a wooden spoon, for 8–10 minutes, until evenly browned. Season to taste with salt.

2. Meanwhile, cook the potatoes in a saucepan of salted boiling water for 15–20 minutes, until tender but not falling apart. Drain, tip into a bowl and mash well, then stir in the cheese until melted. Stir in the beef mixture.

3. Preheat the oven to 200°C/400°F/Gas Mark 6. Brush 2 baking sheets with melted butter. Brush 1 sheet of filo with melted butter, put a second sheet on top and brush with more melted butter. Cut the double layer lengthways into 3 strips. Put a heaped tablespoon of the filling near 1 end of a strip, then fold over the corner to form a triangle. Continue to fold over in triangles to make a neat parcel, then place on a prepared baking sheet. Make 14 more triangles in the same way. Brush with melted butter and bake in the preheated oven for 8–10 minutes, until golden brown. Serve the pastry triangles with a warm tomato and basil salsa.

BEEF & MOZZARELLA RISOTTO BALLS

SERVES: 4

PREP TIME: 30 MINS PLUS COOLING

COOK TIME: 1 HR

INGREDIENTS

300 g/10½ oz long-grain rice
55 g/2 oz butter
2 tbsp grated Parmesan cheese
1 tbsp chopped fresh parsley
1 tbsp olive oil
1 shallot, finely chopped
1 garlic clove, finely chopped
115 g/4 oz fresh beef mince
100 ml/3½ fl oz dry white wine
2 tbsp tomato purée
115 g/4 oz mozzarella cheese, cut into cubes
2 eggs
55 g/2 oz plain flour
sunflower oil, for deep-frying
salt and pepper

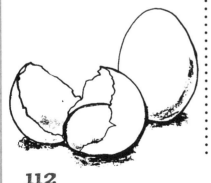

1. Cook the rice in a large saucepan of salted boiling water for 15 minutes, until tender. Drain, rinse with boiling water and return to the pan. Stir in half the butter, the Parmesan cheese and parsley. Spread out on a baking sheet and leave to cool.

2. Meanwhile, melt the remaining butter with the olive oil in a saucepan. Add the shallot and garlic and cook over a low heat, stirring occasionally, for 5 minutes, until softened. Add the beef, increase the heat to medium and cook, stirring frequently and breaking it up with a wooden spoon, for 5–8 minutes, until evenly browned. Stir in the wine and cook for 5 minutes. Reduce the heat and stir in the tomato purée, then cover and simmer for 15 minutes. Season to taste with salt and pepper.

3. When the rice is cold, shape into balls. Make a small hollow in each and put a spoonful of meat mixture and a cube of cheese inside, then re-shape to enclose the filling. Lightly beat the eggs in a dish and spread out the flour in a separate dish. Dip the balls in the egg and then in the flour. Heat enough sunflower oil for deep-frying in a deep-fat fryer to 180–190°C/350–375°F, or until a cube of bread browns in 30 seconds. Cook the balls, in batches, until golden brown, and serve immediately.

RISSOLES

SERVES: 6

PREP TIME: 30 MINS
PLUS CHILLING

COOK TIME: 35–45 MINS

INGREDIENTS

1 kg/2 lb 4 oz potatoes,
cut into chunks

1 onion, finely chopped

500 g/1 lb 2 oz fresh beef mince

1 tbsp snipped fresh chives

1 tbsp chopped fresh parsley

2 tsp Worcestershire sauce or
tomato ketchup

3 eggs

3 tbsp plain flour

175 g/6 oz fresh breadcrumbs

sunflower oil, for shallow-frying

salt and pepper

1. Cook the potatoes in a large saucepan of salted boiling water for 20–25 minutes, until tender but not falling apart. Drain well, tip into a bowl and mash the potatoes until smooth.

2. Add the onion, beef, chives, parsley and Worcestershire sauce and season to taste with salt and pepper. Mix well until thoroughly combined. Cover the bowl with clingfilm and chill the mixture in the refrigerator for 30–45 minutes to firm up.

3. Dampen your hands and shape the mixture into 12 sausage-shaped rissoles. Lightly beat the eggs in a shallow dish, spread out the flour in a second shallow dish and spread out the breadcrumbs in a third shallow dish.

4. Pour oil into a large frying pan to a depth of about 1 cm/½ inch and heat. Meanwhile, coat the rissoles first in the flour, then in the beaten egg and, finally, in the breadcrumbs. Shake off any excess.

5. Add the rissoles to the frying pan, in batches if necessary, and cook over a medium heat, turning occasionally, for 8–10 minutes, until crisp, evenly browned and cooked through. Remove from the pan with a fish slice and keep warm while you cook the remaining rissoles. Serve immediately.

BEEF & MUSHROOM WONTONS

MAKES: 12–15   **PREP TIME: 30 MINS**   **COOK TIME: 15 MINS**

INGREDIENTS

12–15 square wonton wrappers
groundnut oil, for deep-frying

SOY-GINGER DIPPING SAUCE

3 tbsp soy sauce
2 tsp finely grated fresh ginger

FILLING

125 g/4½ oz lean sirloin or rump steak, minced
1 spring onion, green part included, finely chopped
2 button mushrooms, finely chopped
1 small garlic clove, finely chopped
½ tsp finely chopped fresh ginger
½ tsp soy sauce
¼ tsp salt
¼ tsp freshly ground white pepper
⅛ tsp five-spice powder
½ tsp cornflour
1 egg, beaten

1. To make the dipping sauce, combine the soy sauce and ginger in a small serving bowl. Set aside.

2. To make the filling, combine the minced steak, spring onion, mushrooms, garlic and ginger in a bowl. Mix the soy sauce, salt, pepper, five-spice powder and cornflour to a thin paste. Add the paste to the beef mixture, then stir in half the beaten egg. Stir with a fork until very well mixed.

3. Separate the wonton squares and place on a tray, rotating them so one corner is facing towards you. Cover with a clean damp tea towel to prevent cracking. Working with one square at a time, place a slightly rounded teaspoon of filling in the bottom corner 1 cm/½ inch away from the point. Fold the point over the filling, then roll up two thirds of the wrapper, leaving a point at the top. Moisten the right- and left-hand corners with a dab of water. Fold one corner over the other and press lightly to seal into a bishop's mitre shape. Continue until all the wontons are filled.

4. Heat enough oil for deep-frying in a large wok to 180–190°C/350–375°F, or until a cube of bread browns in 30 seconds. Deep-fry the wontons in batches for 4–5 minutes until golden brown. Remove with tongs and drain on kitchen paper. Serve with the dipping sauce.

2

3

4

FAILSAFE FRIENDS!

Once you have chosen and created your tasty dish from the tempting selection of minced meat recipes in this book, you might then be wondering what to serve with the dish to complete your meal. Here are a few quick and simple ideas for accompaniments that go well with some of the recipes, to make your mealtimes even more enjoyable.

• Oven-baked or deep-fried homemade chips are the perfect accompaniment for burgers. Once cooked, season the hot chips lightly with salt and black pepper and serve alongside the burgers. Try serving with Bacon-wrapped Chicken Burgers (page 14) or Pork and Rosemary Burgers (page 32).

• Potato wedges (made with either standard or sweet potatoes) are a great alternative to chips. Serve plain or season them before baking with Cajun seasoning, Jamaican jerk seasoning, lemon or garlic pepper or another seasoning mix of your choice. Alternatively, toss the hot baked wedges with some finely chopped fresh parsley or chives just before serving. Great served with Beef Burgers (page 26) or Turkey Pot Pie (page 16).

• Serve soft cooked polenta (either plain or flavoured with chopped fresh herbs, such as thyme or rosemary, or dried crushed chillies and grated Cheddar cheese) or pan-fried or grilled herby polenta slices, with tasty meatballs and sauce, such as Beef Meatballs with Sichuan Chilli Sauce (page 58).

• Cook basmati rice with flavourings such as cinnamon sticks and cracked green cardamom pods, to make delicious fragrant rice to serve with minced meat dishes (remove the spices before serving the rice). Try serving with Chilli Lamb (page 68) or Chilli Con Carne (page 52) in place of plain boiled rice.

• Add flavour to cooked couscous or bulgar wheat by adding chopped salad vegetables, such as watercress or rocket, spring onions and cucumber, and tossing with a light lemon, herb or chilli dressing. Serve with kebabs/skewers or meatballs and sauce.

• Golden and crisp roasted mixed root vegetables (such as sweet potatoes, celeriac, carrots and parsnips) create a tasty starchy side dish, ideal for serving with dishes such as Meatloaf (page 24).

• Sticky glazed honey-roast beetroot or caramelized roast shallots go well with dishes such as Chicken-stuffed Squash (page 12).

• Toss chunks of prepared vegetables (such as mixed peppers, courgettes and red onions) in some oil, add some chopped garlic and salt and pepper (and a little chopped fresh thyme too, if you like) and roast in a fairly hot oven until soft and lightly charred. Add some cherry tomatoes or plum tomato wedges towards the end of the roasting time. Perfect served with griddled burgers or kebabs/skewers.

• Minted peas and green beans, or green beans with hazelnut dressing, go well with Shepherd's Pie (page 38).

• Sometimes a simple side dish is all you need. Stir-fried greens, wilted spinach with shallots, buttered leeks, a mixed garden or allotment salad, homemade crunchy coleslaw (with sunflower or pumpkin seeds added for extra crunch) or a mixed dark leaf salad with a light and tasty dressing, create quick and easy accompaniments for dishes such as Minced Beef Pizza (page 28), Meatball Risotto (page 36) or Turkey and Mushroom Cannelloni (page 78).

• Instead of plain mashed potato, create other tasty mash by combining and cooking standard potatoes with celeriac, sweet potatoes, parsnips or carrots. Season the hot mash with black pepper and fresh herbs, such as snipped chives or chopped flat-leaf parsley. Great served with meatballs and sauce, or used as a topping for cottage or shepherd's pie, or try serving with Turkey Stroganoff (page 82).

CRISPY PORK DUMPLINGS

Ready-made wonton wrappers make these crispy dumplings a cinch to prepare. As well as a fantastic appetizer, you can also serve as a main dish, allowing around 15 dumplings per person.

MAKES: 20   **PREP TIME: 15 MINS**   **COOK TIME: 5-10 MINS**

INGREDIENTS

3 spring onions, roughly chopped
1 garlic clove, roughly chopped
1 small fresh red chilli, deseeded and roughly chopped
250 g/9 oz minced pork
20 wonton wrappers
groundnut oil or vegetable oil, for deep-frying
salt

1. Put the spring onions, garlic, chilli and pork in a food processor and season with salt. Process to a smooth paste.

2. Remove the wonton wrappers from the packet, but keep them in a pile and cover with a clean, damp tea towel to prevent them drying out. Lay one wrapper on a work surface in front of you in a diamond shape and brush the edges with water. Put a small amount of filling near one edge and fold the wrapper over the filling. Press the edges together to seal the parcel and shape into a semicircle like a pasty. Repeat with the remaining wrappers and filling.

3. Heat enough oil for deep-frying in a large wok to 180–190°C/350–375°F, or until a cube of bread browns in 30 seconds. Add the dumplings, in batches, and cook for 45 seconds–1 minute until crisp and golden brown all over and the pork filling is cooked through. Remove with a slotted spoon, drain on kitchen paper and keep warm while you cook the remaining dumplings. Serve immediately.

SPRING ROLLS

With a tasty pork and prawn filling, these crisp golden rolls are an irresistible starter.

MAKES: 20

PREP TIME: 15 MINS PLUS COOLING

COOK TIME: 25-30 MINS

INGREDIENTS

6 dried Chinese mushrooms, soaked in warm water for 20 minutes

1 tbsp vegetable or groundnut oil, plus extra for deep-frying

225 g/8 oz minced pork

1 tsp dark soy sauce

100 g/3½ oz canned bamboo shoots, rinsed and julienned

pinch of salt

100 g/3½ oz raw prawns, peeled, deveined and chopped

225 g/8 oz beansprouts, trimmed and roughly chopped

1 tbsp finely chopped spring onions

20 spring roll wrappers

1 egg white, lightly beaten

1. Squeeze out any excess water from the mushrooms and finely slice, discarding any tough stems.

2. Heat a wok over a high heat, then add the oil. Add the pork and stir-fry until the pork is cooked through and no longer pink.

3. Add the dark soy sauce, bamboo shoots, mushrooms and a little salt. Stir over a high heat for 3 minutes.

4. Add the prawns and cook for 2 minutes until they turn pink and start to curl. Add the beansprouts and cook for a further minute. Remove from the heat and stir in the spring onions. Leave to cool.

5. Place a tablespoon of the mixture towards the bottom of a wrapper. Roll once to secure the filling, then fold in the sides to create a 10-cm/4-inch piece and continue to roll up. Seal with egg white.

6. Heat enough oil for deep-frying in a large wok to 180–190°C/350–375°F, or until a cube of bread browns in 30 seconds. Fry the rolls for about 5 minutes, until golden brown and crispy.

PORK & CABBAGE GYOZA

MAKES: 24   **PREP TIME: 30–35 MINS**   **COOK TIME: 20–25 MINS**

INGREDIENTS

24 gyoza wonton skins
2 tbsp water, for brushing
oil, for pan-frying
2 tbsp Japanese rice vinegar
2 tbsp shoyu (Japanese soy sauce)

FILLING

100 g/3½ oz Napa cabbage, finely shredded
2 spring onions, finely chopped
115 g/4 oz fresh pork mince
1-cm/½-inch piece fresh ginger, finely grated
2 garlic cloves, crushed
1 tbsp shoyu (Japanese soy sauce)
2 tsp mirin
pinch of white pepper
salt, to taste

1. To make the filling, mix all the ingredients together in a bowl.

2. Lay a gyoza wonton skin in the palm of your hand and place 1 heaped teaspoon of the filling in the centre. Brush a little water around the edges of the wonton skin.

3. Fold the skin sides up to meet in a ridge along the centre and press the edges together. Brush the curved edges of the skin with a little more water and make a series of little folds along the edges.

4. Repeat with the remaining gyoza wonton wrappers and filling. Heat a little oil in a deep lidded frying pan and add as many gyoza as will fill the bottom of the pan with just a little space in between.

5. Cook for 2 minutes, or until browned. Add water to a depth of 3 mm/⅛ inch, cover the pan, and let simmer over a low heat for 6 minutes, or until the wrappers are translucent and cooked. Remove and keep warm while you cook the remaining gyoza.

6. Put the vinegar in a small dipping dish, stir in the shoyu, and add a splash of water.

7. Transfer the gyoza to a serving dish and serve with the sauce for dipping.

LAMB KOFTAS WITH CHICKPEA MASH

SERVES: 4

PREP TIME: 25 MINS PLUS CHILLING

COOK TIME: 25–30 MINS

INGREDIENTS

250 g/9 oz fresh lean lamb mince

1 onion, finely chopped

1 tbsp chopped fresh coriander

1 tbsp chopped fresh parsley

½ tsp ground coriander

¼ tsp chilli powder

oil, for brushing

salt and pepper

CHICKPEA MASH

1 tbsp olive oil

2 garlic cloves, chopped

400 g/14 oz canned chickpeas, drained and rinsed

50 ml/2 fl oz dairy-free milk

2 tbsp chopped fresh coriander

salt and pepper

coriander sprigs, to garnish

1. Put the lamb, onion, herbs, spices and salt and pepper to taste in a food processor. Process until thoroughly combined.

2. Soak 12 wooden skewers in water for 20 minutes to prevent burning. Divide the mixture into 12 portions and, using wet hands, shape each portion into a sausage shape around a skewer. Cover and chill in the refrigerator for 30 minutes.

3. To cook, preheat a griddle pan over a medium heat and brush with a little oil. Cook the skewers in 2 batches, turning occasionally, for 10 minutes, or until browned on all sides and cooked through.

4. To make the chickpea mash, heat the oil in a saucepan and gently fry the garlic for 2 minutes. Add the chickpeas and milk and heat through for a few minutes. Transfer to a food processor or blender and process until smooth. Season to taste with salt and pepper, then stir in the fresh coriander. Garnish with coriander sprigs and serve with the koftas.

INDEX